THE FLINTKNAPPERS' MONTHLY- MAG
APRIL 2020

BY RAY HARWOOD

Published by Spokane Trading Company
2020 Copyright

Permissive use was obtained for all content

ISBN – see back cover

PRINTED IN THE UNITED STATES OF AMERICA
10 9 8 7 6 5 4 3 2 1
First Edition

. Acknowledgements and addendum
The author wishes to extend his thanks and appreciation to
D.C Waldorf, Mound Builder Books, CHIPS Newsletter Archives,
Crow Haven Archives, The Crow's-nest Studio Research Facility
and Archives. PSK members and PSK Archives and website.

WARNING:
Flintknapping is very dangerous and can cause, severe lacerations,
silicosis and many other serious health
Problems including death.
If you do so it is only at your own risk.

Here we are stone age people with stone-age brains in 2020! If you are reading this monthly publication you are like me, born in the wrong millennia. I like rocks, horses and "dawgs" be than modern humans, I am not saying I don't have apathy for or sadness for them or don't feel joy when one of them succeeds, I just don't get along with them. I don't even get along with other flintknappers. That being said I will for the sake of a small readership quote Rodney King, famous for the LA riots "can'y we just get along?"

For this new publication, this will be, by design, monthly. This first few issue will focus on current events, as will the all, but these few will also focus on the history of the craft. Lake a Broadway play bill I will introduce the players that have been instrumental as they weaved in and out of the history of flintknapping. I have hundreds of articles, videos and blogs sI will attempt to put a fresh spin on it.

Flintknapping, according the PSK, is defined as Flintknapping: The art of making stone tools such as arrowheads, knife blades, spear points, atlatl points, scrapers, etc., by remove flakes from conchoidal stone via percussion or pressure flaking. The great and powerful "dean of American flintknapping", Don Crabtree defined a flintknapper as one who forms stone implements by controlling the fracture of the material. An artificer, a stoneworker, using conchoidal fracture. Obsidian bearing well-developed conchoidal (clam-shell-shaped, conch sea shell) fracture with concentric rings, like when you through a rock into still water. A common "bb" hole "cone" fracture in glass is a complete fracture as a conchoidal spall would by a partial. The cone that pops out of the opposite side of the glass from the entry hole of the bb is called the Hertzian cone. That simple cone is the essential component of flintknapping because every flake starts with that cone. The flakes are detached with a percussion blow to a prepared platform with a hammer stone, or pressed of with pressure from a pressure flaking tool. An indirect percussion method is similar to chiseling.

Flintknapping is used by some to create fraudulent artifacts, sell as art, or as a vital tool in the study of flaked stone artifacts, a science known by archaeologists as "lithic technology". Lithic Technology is essentially experimental flintknapping; tool production, use, and maintenance and subsequent analysis

So then about me, not my favorite subject, but relevant none the less. So I will start with the present day and work backwards. The past several weeks I have been in isolation lockdown for a little nasty devil named Covid 19 my wife and I living in separate parts of our house on the Spokane River in North Idaho. Every word the comes out of my mouth is like nails on a chalk board, and I have only a few folks I talk to on the phone, they too are reluctant to pick up the phone at this point, so here I am resolved to be putting my paen to paper to express my flintknapping thoughts.

The phone! So last month I was in my first online knap-in! So is this what online dating is like? Perhaps but the online knap-ins probably have more drama and less blood the online dating. So I was sitting at the table binge eating when the bell mechanism on my cell phone went off. I went to check rather on the spot because I have alienated myself from everyone with right wing political rants LOL. So I looked around the house in a tizzy, flipping over couch cushions, throwing papers with un-legible notes or grocery lists and cussing up a sailors leave "WHERE IS MY GLASSES!?" Almost in tears, I do what no life loving Corona survivor would do, I put my hand over my face as desperate people often do! OH there is my dang glasses, propped up on my forehead like a famous Hollywood actor being cool with his sunglasses. I get the phone and push the button, luckily the battery level is still at a reasonable 25% charge, it locks up at about 15%. So with phone in hand and glasses on I read the tiny letters on the screen that looks smaller every year,
OK it is a message from Gary Picket that seems strange I usually on here from him once a year as he drives from his home in Bakersfield, California to Mercle Hicks' Fine-gold knapin over by Fresno. Most of the time Gary is really buzzy, he works full time helping folks with special needs, he has a beautiful new wife that is having him help around the house and with here business, something to do with spiritual healing I think, when they are not doing that Gay is involved with the local Kern County Museum, and was once the president. He does flintknapping demonstrations at pow wows and puts on a monthly knap-in at Hart Park over by the Kern River plateau. The note is about a group phone knap-in to be help the next day, Sunday. This would take the place of the monthly Bakersfield knap-in, which has been going uninterrupted every month for about twenty years, I image this is some sort of world's record. I have gone to dozens of these, very laid

back with lots of buffalo/bison chili from knapper John Peri. I was there at the first knap-in in Bakersfield and helped "invent it". I was actually surprised to be invited to the group phone knap-in as Gary was quite upset with me for being kicked off a Yahoo-group called the TARP, the brain child of knapper Richard Sanchez. Richard was ill and had to take a break from hosting said group, when he got back to tack it over again, his "friends" would not relinquish it, so he lost his large knapper web group. After Richard the group had gone P.C. and you could only say certain thing that were OK by the host, free speech was gone, yep hosted by the Democrats LOL. Anyway I chimed in on a discussion on "FOG", flake over grinding, saying with was more of an actual lapidary art than true tradition flintknapping. If you look and a caveman knapping and FOG I think you can see what I was getting at. I was not being mean, simply stating the obvious. I love FOG knapping and plan on doing it much more since I have the Jimmy Williams DVD on how Jim Hopper does it. Anyway, I was kicked off the TARP. Funny since I do a lot of lapidary knapping myself in the form of slab knapping. So I get dressed Sunday morning excited for the phone knap-in and step out into the garage and hit the electric garage door opener button on the wall to my left, the door goes up with a wine and groan to reveal a foot of spring sow! I no! I can't be part of this first phone knap-in in history. So eventually it worked and I chimed in with my attendance. Gary and John Peri were chatting away, very familiar voices to my brain. For reasons of silicosis, I strictly do not knap-inside, I have had too many close calls and have lost too many friends to it not to take it seriously. Finely I got sick of just listening and sat next to the open door and knapped in the front of the garage. It was about the same as a real knap-in because you just stare down at your lab and listen to BS LOL. It was not long until I cut myself and went to get a Band-Aid. When I returned to the phone there were several more knapping chipping and chatting and John Peri had left the phone. I finished up a large side-notch point of my favorite rock, Glass Buttes, "Silver Sheen" , less sheen the better, and said my farewells.

This is the same week I had finished up my book about Ted Orcutt, the historic Karuk Indian knapper of Glass Buttes in the late 1800s, so I had just got off the phone with Emory Coons and Cole Hurst, both these knapping knap the giant blades, what Ted Orcutt was famous for. I did extensive recorded interviews with both mega-biface knappers and will have to transcribe them on the next day with bad weather. So I got a lot of the inside scoop of mega knapping, 30 inches long and bigger. Also, I had email conversations from Magwa on the Nez Pierce Reservation and flintknapping pioneer D.C Waldorf. Cole Hurst knaps for certain Native American situations the have sort of sacred knowledge, so I could not use any of his information in the book. Emory's incite from living his entire life at Glass Buttes and being unquestionable master knapper, was an invaluable resource. I finished up the book and uploaded it to kindle books on line and for paperback Amazon books. I was really excited about this, I had done hundreds of hours of research. The book started out at 350 pages, but by the time I took out the Cole Hurst information and the information I had gleaned from Dr. Zach Hurby and Ben Eble, whom I had been conducting research as a team the book was down to about 65 pages. I exactly awaited the email, it came and the formatting ruined the Amazon book, but I published it anyway. It came up the next morning and I excitedly posted it all over the internet social media. Cabin fever was creeping in so I snuck out of my Covet 19 lockdown down and carefully got down to the river and paddled around in my kayak.

When I return I has a one man knap-in in the back yard with a nice BBQ, yum turkey dogs! I watched some Johnny Winter Guitar videos on YouTube and went off to bed. The next morning I plugged in my lousy old laptop and made coffee, I always locks up when I am excited about seeing something or have to get important information. When I finally got onto the data page on my Kindle/Amazon site I could not believe my eyes as they gazed upon the chart "zero sales". I pushed reboot and waited for the little circle to spin on my computer screen. Up came the new visual of the chart, yep! Zero sales. YIKES!

Ok plan "B", send the link to everyone I have ever dealt with on my Yahoo mail account, ha ha, evil grin upon on my face. Real-estate people, doctors' offices, the dentist, the vet,, the VA, my old music band mates, record industry people, Squatch hunting partners you name it LOL. So that next day I did a manic on flintknapping frenzy trying to find a point type and stone that I could mass produce as I had lost my life savings in the last weeks from the Covit 19 market crash. Yes I lost well over 100,000

Bucks, no high rises in north Idaho to jump out the window, so I flintknap instead.

The next morning, sure I beat the system; I went through the stressful morning ritual of getting my old computer online. OK I open my Kindle/Amazon site again and again I could not believe my eyes as they gazed upon the chart "zero sales". I pushed reboot and waited for the little circle to spin on my computer screen. Up came the new visual of the chart, yep! Zero sales. YIKES! No plan "C". "If at first you don't succeed, Try, try, try again". The proverb can be traced back to the writings of Thomas H. Palmer, kept haunting my feeble mind, but I truly was out of options. So this monthly publication will have to do.

The month before I had published the Journal of Lithic Research and to my pleasure it did not do too bad, got onto the data page on my Kindle/Amazon site I could not believe my eyes as they gazed upon the chart and saw several sales a day for several days, mostly for the UK. That first issue was a paper I had written with my old college professor Clay Singer.

In 1982, a series of experiments were conducted to determine something about arrow shaft variability affecting the breakage patterns of projectile points. Thirty identical points were made from fused shale (a local meta-sedimentary $SiO2$), and then hafted to three different types of arrow-shafts: 1) One-piece solid hardwood (Self arrow with the nock cut into the shaft), b) two piece hardwood "footed arrow", hardwood spliced or inserted into the pile end as a fore-shaft, for durability and balance, glued in hardwood nock, and c: two-piece hardwood and cane (also a

footed arrow). The three groups of arrows, ten of each type, were shot at identical wood plank targets with hand held bow from a distance of 25 feet (8 m). More than 90% of the points broke on impact leaving the broken tip imbedded in the plank. Breaks occurred either at the tip or midsection, sometimes accompanied by basal fractures (broken tangs). Both hinge and languette (tongue like projection) fractures were generated but no burinations or spiral fractures occurred in the thirty trials conducted. Fracture type and location appear to be strongly correlated with hafting form and style of shaft. Compound shafts of wood and cane seem to absorb more shock on impact and therefore fewer points are broken. Also, breaks tend to occur closer to the tip with compound shafts. Points with broken tips are easily resharpened and reused, whereas medial breaks usually render the point useless as a projectile point (Knetch 1997, Kelterborn 2001, Titmus and Woods 2006). Broken projectile points from archaeological contexts may be understood more clearly if the cause and mechanisms of use-fracture are better understoodSo my next book project came quite from left field, I didn't even plan it.
WHAT IS FLINTKNAPPING?

Flintknapping, according the Puget Sound Knappers , is defined as the art of making stone tools such as arrowheads, knife blades, spear points, atlatl points, scrapers, etc., by remove flakes from conchoidal stone via percussion or pressure flaking. The great and powerful "dean of American flintknapping", Don Crabtree defined a flintknapper as one who forms stone implements by controlling the fracture of the material. A knapper is an artificer or a stoneworker using conchoidal fracture. Obsidian bearing well-developed conchoidal (clam-shell-shaped, conch sea shell) fracture with concentric rings, like when you through a rock into still water. A common "bb" hole "cone" fracture in glass is a complete fracture as a conchoidal spall would by a partial. The cone that pops out of the opposite side of the glass from the entry hole of the bb is called the Hertzian cone.

The cone is the essential component of flintknapping because every flake starts with that cone. The flakes are detached with a percussion blow to a prepared platform with a hammer stone, or pressed of with pressure from a pressure flaking tool. An indirect percussion method is similar to chiseling. Pressure flaking is the shaping by removing, or chipping off sequential flakes.

I am unsure if this book will be read, because of the current Corona Virus shutdown and quarantines I was unable to contact anyone outside a close nit knapper group. It was a nice afternoon, winter is over an usually I would be out in the north woods I would set out to collect glass and flint to chip into arrowheads, go fishing, back packing or canoeing. Instead, I am laying on my back staring out at the clouds above my roof, only partly obscured by a few very tall ponderosa pines as they dance in the breeze. Some of the clouds resemble animals and sometimes fat ladies. I started the Journal of Lithic research in the last couple weeks to deal with my boredom, but no one bought any copies of Kindle or Amazon to speak of. I went to sleep and awoke just after midnight; April, 24 2020. I had a very lucid dream. In the dream I was up in those funny shaped cloud and I was looking down toward the earth. I could see where the snowflakes being made and fall the great distance down to the earth. I saw the snowflakes from the top down. Curious to see how they were made, as I don't think anyone has every observed this, I fixed my glance that way. My eyes caught a most bizarre image. There sitting in the clouds were two men sitting in cloud chairs, they sat in proximity of a large milk white boulder. As I watched, one man struck the large white boulder with a copper hammer, with each strike a plethora of milk while flakes detached from the boulder and floated down to earth as snowflakes. To my amazement I recognized one the man; it was Richard Warren, one of the early pioneers of knapping. The other man was James Hopper! Why was James Hopper and Richard Warren, master flintknappers, in my cloud dreams? I think when I was a kid my favorite Rolling Stones song was called "Get Off My Cloud", but I imagine I dreamt of the clouds because I had fell asleep watching them float slowly bye. Why James Hopper and Richard Warren? Well I had been studying a video DVD that I had procured from Flintknapper Jimmy Williams). Jimmy Williams is a California flintknapper, known for his research into the Ishi points (Chips Vol.21 No.3) for his Dalton studies (Chips Vol 23, No.3) and for his YouTube programming. The film was produced by Mr. Williams and it was the James Hopper methodology of flake over grinding. Furthermore, Jimmy Williams had emailed me late last year and he wanted to know if the Flintknappers' Hall Of Fame, that I founded, was still active and if anyone had nominated James Hopper. I let Mr. Williams know that, I had not been actively involved in the project for some time after being criticized for it and even threatened. I assured him that I would restart the project among stern objection from the flintknapping community at large. It is my recollection that several knappers had indeed nominated James Hopper for induction into the Flintknappers' Hall of Fame. So to clarify, here is an unanswered letter I sent out after this interpersonal communication with Jimmy Williams concerning the party of one James Hopper; "Hello knappers: Jim Hopper, knapping pioneer, was nominated by many of his knapping colleagues.(most notably , three of you, as were "all ") the current inductees. The only information I have is on the PSK and Lithic Casting lab web-site. Any cool stories or testimonial would be great. I can tell you I started that to start honoring knapper that made significant contributions to knapping, both in history and in modern knapping communities. I try not to dwell on it, but was literally killed in the Army and revived, after that I lived with a lot of mental and physical scars, but on the bright side, I found all the afterlife stuff I heard about is true. Anyway, sorry for the sob story, the relevance is, I was dying about ten years ago or so, my kidneys died and acid ate my joints, I was bed ridden, a friend of mine went out and bought me an old computer, I started using as therapy and typing about stuff I used to like to do and awaited the grim reaper, One of these things I typed out was the Hall of Fame. I did surveys and that is how I came up with the names. One day a friend showed up with a Mexican Curandero (Medicine man) and he treated my dead organs with cactus and corn syrup. That was decades ago, I still have chemical imbalances in my brain and seizures. I tell you, I was hated to the core

for this simple post on my blog, people threatened me and literally hated me deeply for that. And each one that threatened me, I offered to fight them to the death, they all backed down. But I will tell you a story; I have been to three flintknapper funerals where the family listed the dearly departed as an inductee- membership in the "Flintknappers Hall of Fame as one of the most important things on their life list of accomplishments, so let the bastards hate me, I know they have no honor. . So whom that will judge me, so ever, will knap the first stone and cast it at me it at me!"
Hope to hear from you thanks Ray"

Anyhow, I was so inspired by the dream, as soon as I awoke I started working on this article, I called James Hopper and about 3:30 in the morning, he was also wide awake and we conducted the interview at that time.

The DVD is something anyone that want to delve into the world of flintkjnapping should poses and study. Jim Hopper walks the viewer through the intire process of Fog knapping and reveals all the secrets of the trade.

Johnny Winter, was an American guitar hero, singer, Johnny was best known for his high-energy blues-rock performances, these for the most part in the 1960s and 1970s including the Woodstock Music Festival. In 1977, Johnny Winter, a younger blues player, sought out the elder historical blue player Muddy Waters long-time label Chess Records went out of business Johnny Winter brought Waters into the studio to record. This restored the carrier of Chicago blues pioneer and they began a series of great adventures, at the same time they made blues music history with a chain of successful records and concert tours. What does this have to do with FOG knapping you may ask! It is a true story but it is also a parable or analogy of a noble triumph mirroring what happened with James Hopper, and we will get to that in a bit. In this day of the millennial generation, the elders are treated rudely at best, certainly not respected for their experience and knowledge, so when Johnny Winter took his own finances and time to seek out and help aa elder of the community back into the lime light was an exemplary as it were, simply an excellent act of kindness, forethought and respect. Later in life karma came around to Johnny Winter, now he had evolved into the elder statesmen and had been left in the merciless shadows of time. One day an angel of hope came along, a blues guitarist and fan of the elder blues master, Paul Nelson, as Johnny Winter did for Muddy Waters. Paul Nelson did for Johnny Winter and the wheel in the sky keeps on turnin'.

James Hopper, retired and becoming rather isolated from his world of the flintknpping where he was a master and elder lithic statesmen as it were. A living life in the exuberance of trial and error and vast success in the field and to be on Mount Rushmore of the knapping community, to stark isolation, not only because the Corona virus has us locked down, but society has us locked down for our age and ill perceived notion that we are, as elders somehow useless and to be cast aside. But then one day illumination! From out of the light of youth and success flintknapper Jimmy Williams arrives and photons of light shine again on the master, pulled from the shadows of obscurity and put back into the preverbal spot light. James Hopper, has been taken away from his fishing-hole and made whole. Jimmy Williams got James back on the fast track and had him touring the social media with his message of FOG turning a new generation of knappers into perpetrators of the perfectly planned and placed flake scar pattern and using only the stone selected for its glowing beauty. Phase two was to capture the master at his craft and to create a time capsule of place in knapping folklore and history. So Jimmy Williams set out to capture a segment of history lived by his mentor James Hopper, to record a place, and a time and an event of historic significance. Like Edward Curtis, the famous historic photographer whom rushed about the west trying to capture ways of life before they vanished forever. Jimmy Williams is a master of knapping social media and he shared his success and expertise there with James Hopper, but also as Jimmy was doing his vastly popular YouTube channel he also learned how to make a modern style pop culture film. The DVD is a labor of love, quite well done and captures James Harper in his element and in his self-made environment. There James sits, as if there were no one looking, doing what he has done for decades, we are like inert bystanders, the proverbial fly on the wall. Here is where the magic happened and we, as fans or students can now experience it firsthand.

Jimmy Williams had more instore for James and the page turns to new chapter, the one of getting James Hopper the credit and the honorarium he has earned in the lithic art and knapping world. Jimmy contacted me on social media; I suppose I am a bit too controversial or insignificant to be contacted on the phone LOL. The long and short of it was that when I had done the Flintknapping Hall of Fame, James Hopper was somehow and decidedly unfairly left out. He had always been a talking point at my knap-ins, always credited in my articles and newsletters, but here it was a time of resurgence in his style knapping and a time of reelection, our craft developing its own standalone history and hall of honorarium and James Hopper is nowhere to be seen. It is akin to a history textbook leaving out my own great, great, great grandpa Benjamin Franklin, I would be having conniptions. Well in any case Jimmy William nominated his mentor in FOG, this nomination supported Cole Hurst, Emory Coons, and the PSK. James Harper was henceforth abducted into the Flintknappers' Hall Fame. His own mastery and life achievements and tireless efforts of Jimmy Williams, whom I am very proud thankful to, has his rightful place in history. To anyone reading this book, please let me know of anyone you think should be nominated and why. According to Wikipedia "A hall, wall, or walk of fame is a list of individuals, achievements, or animals, usually chosen by a group of electors, to mark their fame in their field. In some cases, these halls of fame consist of actual halls or museums that enshrine the honorees with sculptures, plaques, and displays of memorabilia and general information regarding the inducted recipients.
So with all these failures on my behalf, why do I persevere with this new monthly magazine? Well my guitar had a missing string, and all the guitar stores are locked down as nonessential, so in the morning when it is to cold to kayak, flintknap, or squatch hunt, I type.

, the honorees' plaques may instead be posted on a wall (hence a "wall of fame") or inscribed on a sidewalk (as in a "walk of fame", "walk of stars", or "avenue of fame"). In other cases, the hall of fame is more figurative and consists of a list of names of noteworthy people and their achievements and contributions. The lists are maintained by an organization or community, and may be national, state, local, or private."

The funny thing about the title of this article or chapter is that James Hopper does actually have a number of guitars LOL and was friends with rock guitar pickup legend Seymour Duncan.

So the Jim hopper book came out on Kindle and Amazon the day after I uploaded it, I excitedly opened my data page to see it had sold a few copies, I had done the same thing as the Ted Orcutt but on promotional things. I was fairly happy, but no Jim Hopper, I face booked his page earlier, no like from anyone on the book post, no answer to his messages, and no answer to my phone inquiries? It was strange, there was a complete vacuum from the knapping community, I have been black balled before, but this was eerie! I could see that Jimmy Williams, he did the same thing when I was trying to get information for the book. The next few days, which brings me to now, sales are now zero and I have had not a single comment, well one from Barney DeSimone but I am still confused on what it meant. I titled the book "Lost in the FOG" because it was a nod to James Hopper being the "father of modern FOG knapping". Now it is I that is lost in the fog wondering why I have been black balled by the entire flintknapping community?

So it is on to the next book project. As strange as the book "Lost in the FOG, was from start to finish and then aftermath, a very similar note. D.C Waldorf, "The Way Of The Stone", the flintknapping life story of Dave Waldorf.

Waldorf's book: "Art of Flintknapping" has sold many thousands of copies worldwide and is considered a classic. THE ART OF FLINTKNAPPING, by D.C. Waldorf has been in print since 1975. Over seventy thousand copies sold. It's come to be known as the Flint Knapper's Bible. If you are interested in learning how to work flint in the same manner as Prehistoric Man, this book is for you. It covers the basics such as tools, raw materials, percussion, pressure and indirect percussion flaking, as well as advanced theory. The new Fifth Edition has been updated with appendices covering the use of modern tools such as copper billets as well as more on antler pressure flakers. 80 pages, 8 1/2 X 11", softbound. Over 100 illustrations by Val Waldorf. According to John Whitaker (2007) "The second edition was much more expanded and improved, with illustrations by Val, who is a trained artist. It also received wider publicity, as Callahan reviewed it favorably in Flintknappers' Exchange (1979)". Callahan conveyed to me (1984) that he coached Val in the specifics of flake stone artifact illustrations. He also stated that he used the Art of Flintknapping as his text book for all of his classes in the 1970s and early 1980s. I never had enough flint around to learn his method, but I used to read it and gaze at the photos often. Waldorf also wrote in the original "Flintknappers Exchange" - the classic knapping publication that brought knappers together from academic and folk communities. I met D.C. Waldorf in 1984, through my old newsletter, "Flintknapping Digest"

At eight years old D.C. became interested in Indian traditional technologies. At about fourteen years of age he discovered a nail could pry flakes from the edge of broken glass and flint spalls. Later he found that copper and deer tines worked better for the pressure knapping method. D.C started percussion knapping about 1968 after reading Howell's book "Early Man". H was, at the time one of only a hand full of knappers on the planet. He joined the Archaeological Society of Ohio. His point become so well made that he was banned from selling or displaying them at the meeting.

Waldorf uses antler and stone for percussion and copper and antler for pressure. D.C. and his wife Val took over the "Flintknapping Digest", request, and turned it into "CHIPS" - this was a huge success. He also wrote many other books, including novels out of his rural Missouri cabin. D.C. and Val made a good living with "Mound Builder Books". Later D.C. Waldorf became one of the pioneers of the new Danish Dagger movement. He worked with other dagger knappers on occasion such as Callahan and Stafford. I met D.C. Waldorf in 1983, strictly by phone and snail mail, way before the internet or computers. As I told Dave the other day, I have two regrets in my knapping life, one that I did not go to into Waldorf's world when I was a kid and thereafter, and the other turning down a private demo from Don Crabtree while at his house as a kid. Well the book is being edited and hopefully you will enjoy reading said book.

The inspiration for most academic or research flintknappers came from two sources. Ishi, the Native American knapper, from the historic period of knapping, and Don Crabtree, the current knapper that had rediscovered and mastered the craft, unlocking a multitude of lost technology.

Flint knapping is a part of the world lived in by a very few, but at one time it was part of everyone's world to some degree. The man named Ishi was at the end of that time and the start of this one. It was early in the morning, just the break of dawn, August 9, 1911, some miles south of Red Bluff, California, an exhausted and fearful man was found in the stable of a slaughter house. It was a middle aged American Indian man whom came in from the woods; he was taken off to the jail at Oroville. Sheriff J.B. W Webbe, who was the one who figured out Ishi was a "wild" Indian and locked him up in a cell for the insane, for Ishi's protection more than anything. Curiosity brought both locals and outsiders from miles away to see were described as a "wild-man". Local Indians and "half breeds" came in and attempted to communicate with Ishi, but to no avail. He was the last human on earth that spoke his language. He spoke no English, he was starved and his black hair was burned off short as he was in morning. The man Ishi, the last of the Yahi. The Yahi, a small branch of the Yana, were situated in northern California. Ishi lived in the Mill Creek in the foothills of Mount Lassen, east of the Sacramento River and south of the Pit River. Fortunately for us Ishi was a master flint knapper and he still retained all the knowledge and skill from living a life as his tribe's flint knapping expert. The points Ishi knapped are so delicate, thin and well flaked; they far surpass nearly all points found in archaeological contexts and collections from prehistory. Ishi has a point style named after him, as well as a specific type of flint knapping tool. Ishi had lived his life in the wilderness, his tribe had been wiped out by murderous miners and hunters, Ishi lived alone - isolated. The story of Ishi's capture became headline news. One of the readers happened to be Professors Kroeber and Waterman, anthropologists at the University of California. The two men took an instant interest, as they had gone on an expedition looking for Ishi's people 3 years earlier as some surveyors had happened upon their camp and reported their discovery. It was this discovery that brought the demise of Ishi's people as the surveyors had stolen the Indians' winter supplies as trophies and the Indians did not make it though the winter. Years before the surveyor incident, Indian killers had attacked the tribe of peaceful Indians slaughtering men women and children, one killer switched to his pistol as his riffle was "tearing up the babies too much." You can see why Ishi feared white people; he thought he would surely be executed. Since Ishi's language was extinct, there was no communication with him. It was very discouraging for Ishi and the white men. Finally Waterman broke through with a few Yana words he had found. Ishi went and lived with Kroeber and Watererman at the museum, Ishi would give flint knapping demonstrations every Sunday to crowds of interested onlookers, he also sold his handiwork. On his time off from demonstrations and ethnographic data collecting, Ishi went to the near by hospital and made friends with Dr. Saxton T. Pope, whom was amazed at Ishi's skill as a woodsman and archer. Pope and Ishi went on many trips into the wilderness and Ishi shared his bow making and flint knapping secrets with his new friend. Ishi died at noon, March 25th, 1916. He told his friend Pope at the end "you stay, I go". It was Yahi tradition that the body be buried whole so it could make the trip to the land of the dead, but before Kroeber could do anything about it Ishi's body was autopsied and cremated and his brain cut out and sent to the Smithsonian. California Indians have been trying to gain Ishi's remains for burial but have been largely unsuccessful as no Yahi decedents survive. Just within the last several months, however, a turn of events have taken place and it appears Ishi's remains have been returned to his beloved Deer Creek for a final rest. Don Crabtree was the master knapper of the 1970s, and the link with the academic community. Crabtree, often referred to as "the Dean of American flintknapping". He was born June 8, 1912, in Heyburn, Idaho. According to Harvey L. Hughett, of the University of Idaho: Don spent his early youth in Salmon, Idaho where he first became interested in Indians and their tools. His mother would have him run errands for the next-door neighbor and as a reward this woman would give Don an arrowhead which her husband had gathered. Young Don became fascinated with these tools and even at this early age began to wonder why and how they were made. There were, at this time, many Indians in Salmon. Thanks to Harvey Hughett, at the University of Idaho, whom is now curator of the Don Crabtree Lithic Collection, whom has now moved to Texas, we now know much more about Don Crabtree's childhood. I spoke to Mr. Hughett a few in October of 1999 (Val Waldorf had no problem either) he gave me permission to quote his copyright article on Don Crabtree in Chips Vol. 11, No.3, 1999.: "Young Don became fascinated with these tools and even at this early age began to wonder why and how they were made. There were, at this time, many Indians in Salmon. Their custom was to sit flat on the sidewalk with their legs stretched in front of them. Don found it great fun to jump over their legs and to talk with them, for which he was severely reprimanded by his mother. When Don was six years old, his Family moved to Twin Falls. This was desert country and Don spent most of his time hunting for artifacts, Indian campsites and building his collection of Indian tools. The family's home was just a stone's through from the Snake River Canyon and Don spent every possible moment hunting in the canyon, collecting from campsites and caves and adding to his collection. He also collected obsidian flakes and began to try to reproduce the artifacts. This meant more trips to the canyon for knapping material. Soon, young Crabtree had gathered a fairly large collection of artifacts

and his interest in experimenting with different stones and methods of manufacture to achieve replication increased. He tried many approaches to holding and applying force but with little success and much failure. After interviewing many local Indians, he was disappointed that he was unable to learn anything of how these fascinating artifacts were made. Flintknapping was essentially a lost art even at the time. Don was constantly in trouble with his father for being away from home so much, for the many cuts on his hands and the permanent bloodstains on his clothing. He received many reprimands for coming home after dark. Even this did not cure him of his quest for knowledge of the Native Americans and their tools. At one point, his father became so disgusted with Don spending so much time knapping he offered to pay him $100.00 if he would promise never to make another arrowhead. Don wanted a bicycle and a gun so badly that he considered this offer for some time. However, the love of Indian lore won and he told his father that he could not give up his attempts to make tools as the Indians had. In the late 1930's he was supervisor of the Vertebrate and Invertebrate Laboratory at the University of California at Berkley, this is also where Ishi's artifacts are curated. Also, Ted Orcutt still lived not far to the North. Crabtree also worked in the Anthropology lab with the well known Anthropologist Alfred Krueber, whom were Ishi's friend and caretaker at the museum a few short years before. According to Dr. Errett Callahan (1979), following a flintworking demonstration at a meeting of the American Association of Museums in Ohio, in 1941, Crabtree was employed at the Ohio State Lithic Laboratory with H. Holmes Ellis and Henry Shertrone. He was also advisor in Lithic Studies at the University of Pennsylvania and the Smithsonian Institution's museum. During world war II, Crabtree was coordinating Engineer with Bethlehem Steel in California. Between 1952 and 1962, he was County Supervisor with the U.S.D.A in Twin Falls, Idaho. In 1962 and 1975,
Crabtree was research associate in lithic technology at the Idaho State Museum in Pocatello." Not only was Crabtree a master flintknapper and an inspirational flintknapper , he was also an

expert on the theoretical aspect of stone tool studies. Crabtree published papers on replicative flintworking and other aspects of lithic studies in such publications as:
"American Antiquity" (1939,1968), "Current Anthropology"(1969), "Science" (1968,1970), "Curator" (1970), "Tebiwa" (1964,1966, 1967, 1968, 1972, 1973,1974), and "Lithic Technology" (1975).Crabtree's textbook, "An Introduction to Flintworking", was the mainpublication readily available from 1972 on. The Crabtree book, although 26 years old, is still a classic and is one of the most referenced books in lithic studies today. The book is easy to read and is full of excellent drawings and text. The book is available through the Idaho Museum of Natural History, Idaho State University, Pocatello, Idaho. They also have republished Crabtree's articles, papers, and videos, his articles are better than ours decades later.

Crabtree was featured in many archaeological films in his day, many
were shown around the world in class rooms from elementary school to doctoral classes. These films influence many up and coming flintknappers. The film "Blades and Pressure Flaking" (1969) won best anthropology film at the 1970 American Film Festival. In 1972, the Idaho Museum of Natural History received a grant from
the National Science Foundation for the production of several 16mm
films featuring the legendary flintknapper. Just a few years ago these films were dubbed onto VHS video tape and made available to the
public through Idaho Museum Publications. Though faded somewhat, this footage still maintains its detail and shows Don Crabtree at his
best. In the Shadow of Man, Don is shown quarrying obsidian at Glass Buttes in Oregon. The Flintworker discusses the basics offlintknapping, stone tools are made using simple percussion techniques, and the Hertzian cone theory is introduced. Ancient Projectile Points covers the making of bifacial points. The

hunter's
Edge covers prismatic blade making. The Alchemy of Time concerns heat treating, and the manufacture of Clovis, Folsom and Cumberland points. In 1978, Crabtree had open heart surgery with stone tools. The blades Crabtree made were so sharp that Crabtree's doctor agreed to use them on him after seeing how sharp they were. The first surgery one of Crabtrees's Ribs and a lung section were removed, an 18 inch cut. Crabtree's stone tools were so sharp that there was hardly a scar. Don Crabtree flintknapped all types of artifacts including fluted Folsom , parallel flaking, chevron flaking, notching, blade making and even Ted Orcutt style large obsidian biface points. His large points were very similar to Orcutts , some were so thin that they looked like dinner plates, his obsidian arrow points were very similar to those he helped to curate in Berkley made by Ishi. While working agate Crabtree noticed that his had a satiny texture and the Indian arrowheads out of the same material were like opal.

After much experimentation he rediscovered heat treating of flintmaterials to improve knapping quality. In the later part of his life Crabtree traveled the world meeting and flintknapping with each nation's leaders in lithic fields of endeavor and really opened the door for all of us. During this time flintknapping saw its heyday, "knap-ins", lithic conferences and publications. Sort of what what is happening now but with the academics? Don Crabtree, Dean of American flintknappers, died on November 16, 1980 from complications of heart disease, within six months of Francois Bordes. When Bordes and Crabtree passed away the 1970's academic flintknapping heyday passed away with them.

The Late Don Crabtree, of southern Idaho, is considered to be the "Dean of American Flintknapping" not only for his fine publications, but also for the vast amount of important information he uncovered in a life devoted to the study of stone tools. Don was most probably the first flintknapper in thousands of years to flute a Folsom point, as early as 1941 Crabtree was employed at the Lithic Laboratory at the University of Pennsylvania and the prestigious Smithsonian Institution. He had experimented with fluting in the 1930s but became quite famous for his studies into the Lindenmier Folsom in 1966 . Don Crabtree passed away on November 16, 1980. Jeffery Flenniken and Gene Titmus, students of Crabtree carried on the studies and are still considered to be among the best flintknappers in the world. Don Crabtree was born on June 08, 1912 and died on November 01, 1980 at the age of 68. This person last resided in Kimberly, Idaho in Twin Falls County. D.C. Waldorf's flintknapping idol, François Bordes François Bordes (1919 - 1981) was a French scientist, archaeologist and geologist and was a professor of prehistory and quaternary geology at the Science Faculty of Bordeaux. Bordes changed the approach of prehistoric lithic industries, by introducing scientific and statistical studies in the use of experimental flint knapping. He duplicated some 63 tool types and made over 100,000 stone tools in his life; he also concluded that there were four Neanderthal cultures based on stone tool assemblages. Bordes wrote many books which include the Old Stone Age and A Tale of Two Caves and many articles under the "pen name" Francis Carsac." (Experimental Archaeology) From Wikipedia, the free encyclopedia " François Bordes François Bordes (December 30, 1919 – April 30, 1981), also known by the pen name of Francis Carsac, was a French scientist, geologist, and archaeologist. He was a professor of prehistory and quaternary geology at the Science Faculty of Bordeaux. He deeply renewed the approach of prehistoric lithic industries, introducing statistical studies in typology and expanding the use of experimental flint knapping. He also published many science fiction novels under his pen name. His books have not been translated into English. On the other hand, in USSR the science fiction of Carsac was very popular. He was translated and published into Russian as well as Bulgarian, Lithuanian, Latvian, Hungarian, Estonian amongst others. [edit] Bibliography Prehistory "Principes d'une méthode d'étude des techniques de débitage et de la typologie du Paléolithique ancien et moyen", L'Anthropologie, t. 54 (1950) A Tale of two caves, Harper and Row, 169 p., (1972) Typologie du Paléolithique ancien et moyen, Delmas, Publications de l'Institut de Préhistoire de l'Université de Bordeaux, Mémoire n° 1 (1961), réédition CNRS 1988 : ISBN 2-87682-005-6 Leçons surle Paléolithique, CNRS, 3 vol. (1984) Science fiction Ceux de nulle part (Those from nowhere) (1954) Les Robinsons du Cosmos (The Robinsons of the Cosmos) (1955) Terre en fuite (Fleeing Earth) (1960) Ce monde est nôtre (This world is ours) (1962) Pour patrie, l'espace (For homeland, space) (1962) La vermine du lion (The vermin of the lion) (1967)" According to Ray Harwood's "History of Modern Flintknapping", Errett Callahan read more and more of Bordes's works and met him several times. Francois Bordes stayed at Callahan's house for several days in 1977. Bordes, as Errett, was inspired by Edgar Rice Burroughs and he published numerous science fiction novels. Callahan, as a college student, had once been assigned to be Bordes's escort to a knapping demonstration sponsored by the Anthropology department in D.C. for the Leaky Foundation lectures. In 1977 Bordes spent four days knapping there in Richmond. Bordes had plenty of money to visit the U.S.A. because not only was he a master flintknapper and Europe's leading archaeologist, but also one of the most popular science fiction writers in France. According to Callahan Bordes wrote dozens of novels under the pen name of Franci Carsac. Callahan was influenced quite a bit by Bordes. At the same time Errett was also reading the works of Don Crabtree. Errett was Fascinated by Crabtree, they met in Calgary in 1974 and Crabtree gradually became a heavy influence on Errett's knapping. J.B. Sollberger was another major influence and led Errett to bigger and better things than he could have without that input. Gene Titmus of Idaho, a friend of Crabtree was also a major influence on Callahan, mostly his notching and serrating techniques. Errett stayed in close contact with Gene for many years, Gene a master knapper of percussion and, like Don, about the nicest and humblest guy he'd ever met. Some other overseas influences on Errett were Jacques Pelegrin and Bo Madsen. Pelegrin had been Bordes number one student in France, working under him for years. Pelgrin first trained with Bordes over six summers, for three weeks each summer. Pelegrin worked with a hardwood billit, which he learned to use from Bordes's friend in Paris, Jacques Tixier, whom was one of the Masters of flintworking of the time. Pelegrin became very good with boxwood. Jacques Pelegrin's father built a cottage in the French woods, here Jacques reflected on archaeological concepts and flintknapping. At this time, in the 1970s, Pilegrin was writing a bit back and forth to Master Don Crabtree in the USA and Jacques had begun to read and interpret Crabtree's publications. Pelegrin did public flintknapping demonstations in the Archeodrome, which is on the main road between Beaune and Lyon, France. He is concidered one of the best flintknappers in the world. Pelegrin and Bordes learned English together and spend years flintknapping together and learning, master and student became knapping partners. Jacques Pelgrin went through almost all the Paleolthic French technologies while learning his craft- Levallois, blade making, different kinds of Paleolithic tools, different kinds of flint cores, and leave points, including Solutrean pressure material. It is an interesting fact that Pelegrin learned to flintknap standing up and only changes after his first exposure to other knappers and text. Crabtree died on November 16, 1980 from complications of heart disease, within six months of Francois Bordes. When Bordes and Crabtree passed away the 1970's academic flintknapping heyday passed away with them .It was Francois Bordes that realy put flintknapping on the world map. Bordes was internationally known for having studied and recreating ancient stone tools from 12,000 years ago. Bordes duplicated some 63 tool types. Bordes made over 100,000 stone tools in his life. He was born in France in 1919. Bordes was director of the Labratory of Quarternary Geology and History at the University of Bordeaux, France. Bordes concluded that there were four Neanderthal cultures based on stone tool assemblages. Francois Bordes was an accomplished fellow. He wrote many books which include the Old Stone Age and A Tale Of Two Caves. He wrote several books and many articles under the "pen name" Francis Carsac. Bordes was a hot tempered fellow, with a massive brain and bank account to match, he often visited America and his friends; Don Crabtree, Errett Callahan and Bruce Bradely. Francois Bordes died on April 30th, 1981 while lecturing at the University of Arizona at Tuson

According to Bruce Bradley "François Bordes spent a whole semester at U of A in spring 1970 and he and I spent most every spare moment knapping in a little room on the ground floor of the Anthro building. I still don't know why it was, but he and I hit it off extremely well (pun intended). Our temperaments were absolute opposites. I was born with patience (in knapping) and a high threshold of frustration. When something went wrong and I screwed up I would, for the most part, shrug my shoulders and toss the offending pieces over my shoulder and quietly begin over. François on the other hand was a 'power knapper' and what he lacked in finesse he made up for in sheer force. You can imagine how this worked with the brittle obsidian we had to work with. There was an almost unbroken string of obscenities wafting out of that little room and bouncing around the halls of the Anthro. building. One of François's favorite sayings was "Flint, she is a woman, obsidian, she is a whore". I learned how to swear in 14 languages! A skill I seldom employ, but on rare occasions I can still be heard mumbling unintelligibly some of those colorful phrases. François invited me to participate in his middle paleolithic excavations in SW France that summer and I spent several glorious months digging in 50,000 year old sites, knapping incredible flint (mostly Bergerac), and exploring the countryside and backwoods of the Dordogne. During this time, I once again met up with Jacques Tixier who invited me to come to Lebanon and dig with him near Beirut. This I couldn't pass up and I went there in September 1970. Although I was there only a short three weeks, I managed to have some great adventures and discovered the amazing light pink flint of the Baka Valley. On the way home, I visited a French Canadian archaeologist who I worked with in France, in Cambridge, England. There I was introduced to the rich blue-black flints of the European chalks. I managed to visit the famous Brandon gunflint knapping areas and saw Grimes Graves, the Neolithic flint mining complex. All the while I continued knapping at every possible opportunity."

The Thinking Man: One of the most knowledgeable and talented flintknappers of our time was a Virginia Flintknapper, whom has influenced hundreds, if not thousands, Errett Callahan. We can sit and wonder where Callahan came from and why he was such an influence.

The answer is this, Callahan came into knapping with a great deal of

The International Flintknappers ' Hall of Fame and Museum is encouraging individuals of all ages to "Be A Superior Example," through a new education program as part of a new curriculum to promote healthy habits, while encouraging everyone to live free of drugs and other such substances or vices. It serves as the central point for the study of the history of flintknapping in the United States and beyond, displays flintknapping-related artifacts and exhibits, and honors those who have excelled in the craft, research/ writing, promoting events, and serving the knapping community in an ethical and wilderness loving manner. skill, intellegence and strength, at a time when a whole new generation of archaeologists were coming out of the old school with a lot of questions. Crabtree had just released his book and was bumping out students by the bus load. Archaeology was hungry and Callahan was just what the doctor ordered. He had fresh ideas and an uncanny knapping ability intertwined the craft and theory like no one before or since. In 1956, just out of high school, Errett spent the summer in Yellowstone National Park working at the Old Faithful general store. He was exposed to a lot of history at the park and had access to obsidian, this gave him the start he needed and he began knapping seriously then and has been doing it full steam ever since, later combining his early grinding methods as part of his flaking strategy. It started on a trip out when he was waiting for the train in Montana. He went into a local library and found a book on various point types. He was fascinated by this and it sort of plugged some into his memory. In his spare time he would try to duplicate these, using small pieces of obsidian and bottle glass and guided only by the flintknapping picture in Holling's book. It was another 10 years before Errett realized that there were other people flintknapping. Up until then he thought he was the only one. Errett read more and more of Bordes's works and met him several times. Francois Bordes stayed at Callahan's house for several days in 1977. Bordes, as Errett, was inspired by Edgar Rice Burroughs and he published numerous science fiction novels. Callahan, as a college student, had once been assigned to be Bordes's escort to a knapping demonstration sponsored by the Anthropology department in D.C. for

the Leaky Foundation lectures. In 1977 Bordes spent four days knapping there in Richmond. Bordes had plenty of money to visit the

U.S.A. because not only was he a master flintknapper and Europe's leading archaeologist, but also one of the most popular science fiction writers in France. According to Callahan Bordes wrote dozens of novels under the pen name of Franci Carsac. Callahan was influenced quite a bit by Bordes. At the same time Errett was also reading the works of Don Crabtree. Errett was fascinated by Crabtree, they met in Calgary in 1974 and Crabtree gradually became a heavy influence on Errett's knapping. J.B. Sollberger was another major influence and led Errett to bigger and better things than he could have without that input. Gene Titmus of Idaho, a friend of Crabtree was also a major influence on Callahan, mostly his notching and serrating techniques. Errett stayed in close contact with Gene for

many years, Gene a master knapper of percussion and, like Don, about the nicest and humblest guy he'd ever met. Some other overseas influences on Errett were Jacques Pelegrin and Bo Madsen. Pelegrin had been Bordes number one student in France, working under him for years. Pelgrin first trained with Bordes over six summers, for three weeks each summer. Pelegrin worked with a hardwood billit, which he learned to use from Bordes's friend in Paris, Jacques Tixier, whom was one of the Masters of flintworking of the time. Pelegrin became very good with boxwood. Jacques Pelegrin's

Father built a cottage in the French woods, here Jacques reflected

on
archaeological concepts and flintknapping. At this time, in the 1970s, Pilegrin was writing a bit back and forth to Master Don Crabtree in the USA and Jacques had begun to read and interpret Crabtree's publications. Pelegrin did public flintknapping demonstations in the Archeodrome, which is on the main road between Beaune and Lyon, France. He is considered one of the best flintknappers in the world. Pelegrin and Bordes learned English together and spend years flintknapping together and learning, master and student became knapping partners. Jacques Pelgrin went through almost all the Paleolthic French technologies while learning his craft- Levallois, blade making, different kinds of Paleolithic tools, different kinds of flint cores, and leave points, including Solitarian pressure material. It is an interesting fact that Pelegrin learned to flintknap standing up and only changes after his first exposure to other knappers and text. Bo Madsen is Denmark's premier flintknapper, a grand- master of the Danish art. Madison is an expert on Danish lithics and earned his Ph.D. at Arhus in Jutland, Denmark. Madsen's dagger research influenced Callahan greatly and this spread to America and in this era many knappers were attempting dagger production: Waldorf, Patten, Stafford, Flenniken and Callahan in particular. Errett spend a good deal of time in the 1970s in Scandinavia and returned again in August of 1984. Madsen had moved over to the University of Arhus and was teaching a talented portage, Peter Vemming Hansenat at the University of Copenhagen, the two had co-wrote and published a paper on the replication of square- sectioned axes. While in Scandinavia Callahan gave several flintknapping workshops sponsored by the Archaeological Institute of the University of Uppsala, Sweden, he was assisted by Bo Madsen and Dr. Debbie Olausson. According to Callahan, the Copenhagen area has several talented non-academic knappers as well Thorbjorn Peterson, Asel Jorgensen, and Soren Moses. In later years Errett's biggest influence was Richard Warren. Richard was completely underground and out of contact for most of his knapping life, he became a lapidary knapper that had an exclusive clientele. Rich-

ard Warren's work was incredibly precise, much more than anyone at the time thought was possible. Errett had to reconstruct the Warren technique entirely from scratch. Richard Warren showed Errett there is one important thing: perfection is possible- and that's all he needed to know. Richard Warren died a few years ago, Warren's curiosity was to know what could be done with flint if someone picks up where the best stone age knappers abandoned the craft for metal technology or extinction. In short Richard's quest was for knapping for the sake of art-perfection, by any means possible. Richard used the term "Teleolithics" (FOG) to describe what we now call lapidary knapping, flake over grinding (lap-knapping). After Hannus' colon operation, in 1983, for which Errett made the obsidian blades used in the surgery and observed the entire operation, two of Callahan's students decided to start a company with him to market these blades to the medical community. The one who was supposed to do the marketing dropped out and little became of " Aztecnics". Errett markets his obsidian art through "Piltdown Productions" in Virginia. Callahan is best known for his published work The Basics Of Biface Knapping In The Eastern Fluted Point Tradition A Manual For Flintknappers And Lithic Analysts. This was published in Archaeology Of North America, . He has also published many other books and articles. Including: "Flintknappers' exchange" (the original journal), "The Emic Perspective" and "Flintknapping Digest". The Basics Of Biface knapping In The Eastern Fluted Point Tradition was the single most influential lithic book ever written. The Callahan biface book is Vol. 7, No. 1 of the journal Archaeology Of Eastern North America. The book introduced many new techniques for the study of stone tools, for standard and experimental archaeology. The concepts, "the lithic grade scale, and biface staging, are widely used in flintknapping circles to the point the most new knappers didn't even know these concepts were fairly new and discovered by Callahan. As Crabtree before him Callahan was the only living flintknapper with the confidence to have major surgery done with stone tools he crafted himself. According to the news release on December 9th, 1998, Errett Callahan had major surgery done to repair his right rotator cuff tendon. The two hour landmark operation was done by Dr. Jay Hopkins of Blue Ridge Orthopedics at Lynchburg General Hospital. Callahan's rotor cuff tendon had become completely torn off the top of his humerus bone and had to be extensively reworked. Dr Hopkins said that it was as bad a tear as he had ever witnessed. All incisions were made with Callahan's obsidian scalpels. Dr. Hopkins, after performing the operation, was impressed with the great reduction of bleeding in the initial incisions and states: I used the obsidian blade for a shoulder operation and found them quite satisfactory. They performed very much like a scalpel and the bleeding with the first cut through the skin was minimal. Healing appears to be very much normal, if not accelerated.

Errett Callahan was founder and president of the Society of Primitive

tive

Technology for many years . The Society is an international organization devoted to the preservation of a wide range of primitive

tive

technologies. The SPT preserves and promotes this knowledge-principally by means of a remarkable magazine, the Bulletin of Primitive Technology. Errett has now retired from his editor and chief and president but he will stay an active member. For more information contact Society of Primitive Technology, P.O. Box 905,

Rexburg, Id 83440. The Bulletin is now being edited and produced by

Primitive skills expert, David Wescott. At this time Errett Callahan was in the midst of writing a major book on flintknapping – everything he knows...and he knows a lot..The book is going to focus a on Danish daggers. The book is addressed was both the archaeologist and flintknapper alike. This book was a 20-year research project in which200 daggers were replicated. The research was funded by a grant from the King of Sweden and by Uppsala University. Callahan is co-writing the book with Jan Apel, a PhD student at Uppsala and fellow flintknapper. The new book will do for daggers what his biface book did for that field. Callahan is also working on a book on experimental archaeology.

Callahan used to put on his weeklong classes at Cliff Side on flintknapping, traditional archery, primitive pottery, lithic analysis, and more. Bob Verrey, a former student and longtime flintknapper, archaeologist and supplier of knapping tools offered a scholarship to the school but it is very competitive. Dr. Callahan passed away recently, so he now knaps with his friends in the afterlife.

The Puget Sound Knappers CODE OF ETHICS:

The Puget Sound Knappers will not condone, encourage or sanction the following activities:

The sale of prehistoric artifacts.

Alteration of prehistoric sites.

Sale of modern replicas as authentic prehistoric artifacts.

The sale of modern replicas which do not clearly display permanent marks to distinguish the replicas as modern.

The leaving of a knapping area without policing the debitage, dating and burying it with coins, cans, etc.

Digging or collecting artifacts in a known prehistoric site.

Closures from Covet 19:

All knap-ins, entire world

All museums, entire world

All rock shops, except online, entire world

All rock shows, entire world

See you next month for up-dates or see the PSK web site and social media sites. STAY WELL